Good Night, Sleep Tight!

21 Bedtime Stories & Poems

Nalini Sorensen

Illustrated by Doodlenerve

Designed by Shamika Chaves

HarperCollins*Children'sBooks*

For Neilssss,
How I wish, how I wish you were here.
Sleep well, my big brother. I'll see you on the other side.
– Nalini

First published in 2023 by HarperCollins Children's Books
An imprint of HarperCollins Publishers India
Building No 10, Tower A, 4th Floor, DLF Cyber City, Phase II,
Gurugram – 122002

2 4 6 8 10 9 7 5 3 1

P-ISBN: 978-93-5699-401-0
E-ISBN: 978-93-5699-402-7

Illustrated by **Doodlenerve**
Designed by **Shamika Chaves**
Typeset in Lora Regular 15.5pt/ 27 by **Shamika Chaves**

Printed and bound at Nutech Print Services - India

HarperCollinsIn

Contents

1

Extraordinary

He was born into an extraordinary family. His amma was an extraordinary author. His appa was an extraordinary pianist. And Sunaina, his elder sister, was an extraordinary swimmer.

But Adi felt ... ordinary.

He was an ordinary reader. An ordinary dancer. An ordinary football player. An ordinary cricketer. He drew ordinary cards, and he wrote ordinary stories.

He felt sad that he was not extraordinary. He wanted to be more than just ordinary. Which was why he spent quite a bit of his time being by himself, and not really smiling a lot. Yes, Adi kept to himself mostly. He didn't need anyone else in his life showing him how absolutely ordinary he was.

One day, when he returned from school, his home was filled with excitement.

'Look at the colours,' said Amma.

'What do we feed it?' asked Sunaina.

'Here he is!' exclaimed Appa, excitedly, as Adi entered the room.

Adi walked in, and stopped dead in his tracks. There was the most beautiful parrot chirping loudly, on a perch, right there in the middle of the room looking at him through black, unblinking eyes.

'It is for you, Adi,' said Sunaina.

'For me?' he asked, eyes widening.

'Yes, for you,' Amma replied. 'Haven't you been asking for a pet? Well, you've got one now.'

'It is ... She is beautiful. But ... but where is she from?' asked Adi, softly.

'A flock of them sit by Mira Aunty's window every day. She caught one,' replied Amma, shrugging her shoulders just a little and blowing the hair off her forehead. 'What should we name her?' she continued, breaking Adi out of his trance. Adi shook his head and blinked.

‘Such a vivid green. Let’s call her Hara,’ Adi answered, still staring at the cage in wonder.

‘Here’s how to clean her cage,’ Appa said. ‘You need to clean it once a day. Pull the tray out carefully, roll on the newspaper, fold the edges and push it back in. See? Like this.’ Adi nodded.

‘And to feed her, you open the door carefully, slip your hand in and remove both bowls. Water in the blue one, seeds in the green one. Just one measure of the teaspoon of seeds each day. Easy-peasy, right?’ Appa continued.

Over the next few weeks, Adi took care of Hara exactly as he was taught. He couldn’t be happier. He spoke to her and, when she chirped back, he was quite sure Hara had understood exactly what he had said.

One morning, Adi woke up to unusually loud sounds from the cage. He stretched his body out, arms over his head, then got out of bed and leant his head over to see what all the noise was about. Right outside his window were other parrots, and Hara appeared to be having a conversation with them. Adi watched them chatter. He crept out of bed to get Amma, Appa and Suni. 'I love their chitter-chatter,' he whispered to Suni, as they stood at the door and watched the flock of green birds.

This soon became a regular occurrence. The parrots would arrive at his window and Adi would watch Hara chat with them like long-lost friends.

Adi often wondered what their conversations were about. *Was Hara trying to describe the sound of the telephone? The taste of the store-bought seeds? Appa's music on the piano?*

Were the parrots outside describing their flight past the mountains that morning? The smell of the grass as it was being cut? The feel of the cool breeze as they soared over the ocean in the sky? The falling raindrops? Were they asking Hara to join them outside again?

Adi wondered and wondered. The more he thought about it, the sadder it made him.

One morning, as Adi woke up to the chirping of Hara and her friends, he felt something stir in his heart. He walked quickly to the cage and opened the tiny metal door. It made a small creaky sound as it swung open.

It took Hara a few minutes to realize that the cage door had been opened. She peeked out nervously, a little unsure of herself. Then she gently hopped on to the ledge of the window. She turned once to look back at Adi and, in the blink of an eye, she was off.

Adi watched her fly towards the mango tree across the street, until she disappeared into its green leaves and branches. He stared hard, but he could not see her anymore. The greens had all merged. Leaves and bird became one from the distance.

When Adi sat down to breakfast that morning, he was quieter than usual. 'What's the matter, Adi?' asked Amma.

'I set Hara free, Amma,' Adi replied. 'She has flown away from our home.'

'But why, Adi?' Appa asked, looking surprised, folding the newspaper and pushing his reading glasses back on his nose.

‘Because she wanted to be with her friends. She wanted to feel the breeze and raindrops again as she flew in the sky,’ Adi answered.

‘But … but you loved her,’ said Sunaina.

‘I did. I do,’ said Adi, blinking back tears. ‘But she is happier with her friends.’

‘Oh Adi!’ said Amma, gathering him in a hug. ‘You are so kind. So extraordinarily kind.’

‘Really. So extraordinarily kind,’ echoed Appa.

‘I’m not sure what to say, here. Yes, you are far kinder than I am. Truly extraordinary,’
said Sunaina.

Adi stared at his family. And then he smiled.

Bigger and brighter than ever before in his life.

They would never know how much the word meant to him.

2

The Beach

The beach is my favourite
Place to be,
It's got sand,
And it's got the sea.

I love to scoop up
A fistful of sand,
And watch it trickle,
From hand to hand.

I love to build,
Sand castles too,
And dream about
Animals to rescue.

I love to bury,
My legs in the sand,
And watch as it falls off,
When I stand.

Then there's
The big blue sea,
It looks so inviting
To little me.

I love to swim in it
With my dad,
He says that makes me
A very, strong lad.

I love to sail,
In a bouncy boat,
The breeze cools my face,
As we stay afloat.

And with the round
Setting sun,
I see red, yellow and orange,
All together in one.

It's beautiful to watch,
It's a painting in the sky,
So calm and relaxing,
On the eye.

The beach is my favourite
Place to be,
I think God made it
Just for me.

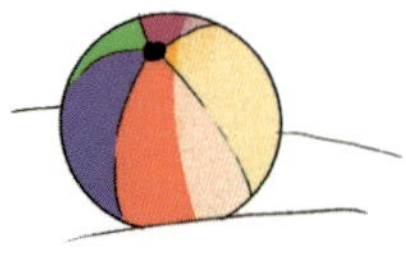

3

How to Get a Good Night's Sleep

You must first make Ma read you a story. Take your time choosing which story you want to hear. It must be long, but not too long. Lie close to Ma, and listen to the story as she reads it. You, of course, know the words by heart, so be alert in case Ma skips a page or two. (Ma often does this.)

As soon as Ma finishes the story, you must impatiently say, 'Again!' If Ma says, 'No, it's late. It's bedtime now,' look as though you are going to cry.

Ma will read it a second time. Guaranteed.

When Ma turns off the light and starts to leave your room, make a 'Hmmmm'—a sleepy sound. Ma will turn back and look at you with a loving smile.

Wait for five minutes, then jump off your bed, and leave your room.

When Dada squints at you from the dining table and asks, 'What are you doing up?'

Quickly reply with, 'I urgently need to use the toilet, Dada.'

Ma will look angry at this. Run fast towards the toilet. Make it really seem urgent.

Once you wash your hands and come out from

the toilet, allow Papa to hold your still slightly wet hand, and lead you back to your bed.

Ask Papa, 'Papa, will you read me a story? Please?'

When Papa makes an excuse, look as though you are going to cry. Papa will read you a story. Guaranteed.

Papa does not skip pages. He never ever does. You are safe to lie down, relax, close your eyes and enjoy the story.

As soon as Papa finishes and reaches forward to turn off the light, give him a sleepy smile. Papa will look back from the door with a loving smile, before he leaves your room.

Wait for five minutes. Then yell out, 'Ma! Ma!'

Once Ma comes inside your room, say, ‘I need your special warm, yellow milk magic, Ma. I can’t sleep.’

When Ma brings the cup with the warm milk, snuggle up close to her. Hold the cup between your hands, bend your head forward and take a deep breath. Inhale the golden goodness that is in the cup.

Ask Ma, ‘What’s in it again, Ma?’

Watch Ma’s face light up as she says, ‘A cup of warm milk, a teaspoon of turmeric, a dollop of honey and a big pinch of my love. All mixed together, just for little you.’

Make sure you drink every last drop of it. This is important. It makes your tummy feel warm and full of love.

When Ma turns off the light and starts to leave your room, make a 'Hmmmm'—a sleepy sound. Ma will look back at you, from the door, with a loving smile. Guaranteed.

After Ma leaves, creep out of bed and bring Teddy, Mimi and Kiara on your bed. Arrange them so that Teddy is to your right, Mimi is to your left and Kiara is in the space above your pillow, between your pillow and the headboard. Give them each a loving pat on their cheek.

Wait patiently for Ma, Papa and Dada to finish watching the news on TV. Listen carefully as they turn off the TV, and the lights and fan, one after the other.

Lie still as each of them come to your room to watch you sleep.

Now this is important:
Do NOT smile even when Ma says things like, 'She looks like such an angel when she sleeps.'

Do NOT flutter your eyelids. Dada normally notices things like that.

Make sure your tummy moves nice and evenly.

Wait for fifteen minutes. Then slowly, slowly, S-L-O-W-L-Y creep into Ma and Papa's bedroom. Slip into their bed as gently as possible. Try not to pull too much of the quilt over you.

Lie still, and keep your eyes firmly closed, as Papa carries you back to your own bed.

Wait for fifteen minutes. Then slowly, slowly, S-L-O-W-L-Y creep into Dada's bed.

Dada is fast asleep.

Turrrrrr-turrrrrr-turrrrrr, Dada snores. It is loud, but not too loud, and the bed gently shakes as he snores.

Lie still on Dada's bed. Then gradually snuggle up closer to him. Tug the sheet over you. Feel the bed rocking you to Dada's snores.

Count the *Turrrrr-turrrrr-turrrs* coming out of Dada's open mouth. Watch as your hand goes up and down on his tummy as he snores.

Before you can reach ten, you will be fast, fast asleep.

You will only wake up when the sun shines in the morning. Guaranteed.

(Turn the page to see where Ma and Papa will find you in the morning.)

ZZZ

4

Eight Hairy, Scary Legs

I'm a spider with eight legs,
That are ever so hairy,
It's part of what makes me,
Really, really scary.

I love my hairy legs,
They're my best feature,
They help me run quick,
And catch an unsuspecting creature.

But it's the start of winter,
And my leggies feel itchy,
It's cold, and they're dry,
And they feel all twitchy.

I wander through the jungle,
And who should I see?
Mr Owl up there,
Staring down at me.

'Errr Owl? Mr Wise One?
Can you help me?
My legs are all itchy,
And white, can you see?'

I stretch my legs out,
Before his unblinking eyes,
And wait for his answer,
Which comes as a surprise ...

'Is this a joke?' he yells,
His eyes bulging out,
'For dry legs, you hairy fool,
Bathe from the waterspout!'

I scamper away,
In the blink of an eye,
Water! I should have thought of that!
Why didn't I? WHY?

I go to the waterspout,
And bathe myself,
Still upset with Mr Owl's tone,
What does he think of himself?

I lie under the spout,
And let the cold water trickle,
Problem solved, I think,
I'm out of this pickle.

I stretch my legs out,
Long on each side,
These should be good as new now,
I think with pride.

But no! They're a mess!
They're wet and shivery,
I try to run, they shake harder,
I look all quivery!

What's a spider to do,
With legs that are shaky?
My eights are still white,
And now even flaky.

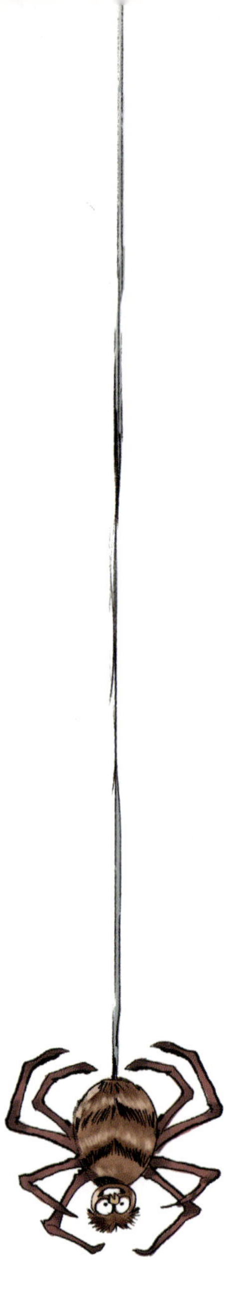

As I lie down in defeat,
Who should come by?
Mr Crow cawing loudly,
I cover my face ... and sigh!

'What's up, oh Hairy?
Why the big grouchy frown?
What is it exactly,
That's got you down?'

I look up. I sigh again.
I'm not sure what to say ...
I sigh once more and admit,
'It's been a really bad day.'

'I went to the wise owl,
About my legs that were dry,
I've bathed in water, like he said,
Now they're wet and shivery,' I sigh.

'The owl? Seriously?
You've got to be joking!
His wisdom's so overrated!'
Crow's loudly croaking.

‘You need advice,
You come to me, ME!
Crows are the cleverest,’
He caws out, with glee.

‘That’s great. But now focus.
My legs that are wet? And flaky?
Any cure? Any solution?
To make them less shaky?’

‘Of course, you hairy fellow!’
He caws louder and louder,
‘For wet, shaky, eight legs,
You’ve got to use powder!’

‘Powder! My goodness!
Thank you, clever crow!’
I laugh as I see,
Crow’s face start to glow.

'You're welcome, oh Hairy!
I'm glad I set the record straight ...'
I slip away as Mr Crow,
Caws on till daybreak.

I slip to a dark corner,
I sprinkle, I dust,
I powder my eights,
In Mr Crow I trust.

I stretch my legs out,
Long on each side,
These should be good as new now,
I think with pride.

But no! They're a mess!
They're sloppy and gloopy,
They slip and stick down,
Now I look all droopy!

What's a spider to do,
With legs that just slip?
I'm not fast and not scary!
My chin starts to dip.

I look down at the mess,
And I start to cry,
When who should be
Swinging on a tree right by?

It's Monkey, my best friend,
With his big smile and long tail,
Ooh-ooh-aah-aah-ing,
His musical scale.

'What's up dear friend?
Why the big grouchy frown?
What is it exactly,
That's got you down?'

I look up. I cry more.
I'm not sure what to say ...
I sniff loudly, all red-nosed,
'It's b-b-been a really b-b-bad day.'

'I w-w-went to that wise owl,
About my legs that were d-d-d-dry,
I've bathed in w-w-water,
But they got wet and shaky!' I cry.

'Then c-c-crow flew b-b-by,
And told me to p-p-powder,
I did! And look, L-L-LOOK!'
I cry louder and louder.

Monkey looks serious,
(not a very common sight),
He scratches his head,
And thinks of Spider's plight.

He scratches some more,
Then clicks his fingers,
'My goodness! I've got it!
I'm the jungle's best thinker!'

'Spidey! Dear Spidey!'
Monkey's eyes shine and gleam,
'For dry legs, you know,
You've got to use cream!'

We buy a big bottle,
With a bright orange squirt,
Of a sweet-smelling cream,
That oozes out with a splurt.

I rub and I dub,
I massage the cream in,
Problem solved, I hope,
With one scary grin.

I stretch my legs out,
Long on each side,
These should be good as new now,
I think with pride.

And yes! Yes indeed!
They're as good as new,
Hairy and scary,
And well-oiled too!

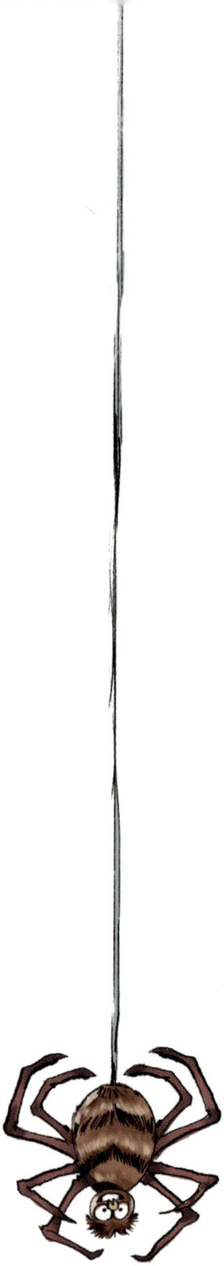

I laugh and I flex,
My very best feature,
They help me run quick,
To catch an unsuspecting creature.

Just then I hear,
A beat and a tune,
I turn to see Monkey,
Start to croon ...

'When it starts to get cold,
And your legs start to dry,
Just cream them dear Spidey,
And you can zip by.'

5

Perfect Penny

Penny loved to dress up. Not the kind of dress-up that you are thinking of. No, not costumes, not make believe.

The real kind.

She loved to wear nice dresses. Nice skirts. Nice trousers. Nice blouses. Nice socks. Nice shoes. Nice bangles. Nice clips in her hair. Nice hats. Nice handbags. Nice necklaces.

She made sure she was always well dressed; that every hair was in place, and that her clothes always matched. Everything was always perfect. She was the most perfectly dressed girl in her class, even in her school uniform.

Every. Single. Day.

She loved receiving compliments from her friends and family ...
'That's such a pretty colour on you!'
'Those shoes are gorgeous!'
'Your hair looks like it was done in a salon!'
'Is this a new skirt? It is beautiful!'

On Saturday evening, Penny left for Aditi's birthday party dressed impeccably, as usual. Her hair was perfect, her dress was perfect and her shoes were perfect. Aditi's mummy planned the best, most fun

parties. Each year was always more fun than the previous one.

When she arrived, the party was already in full swing in the garden. It was a pirate-themed party this year and she could hear the laughter and noise as she walked in. Arun and James had their eye patches on and were sword fighting with balloon swords, Nayantara had a bandana tied on her head, and was walking the plank, Mia was getting a tattoo painted on her arm by a tattoo artist. The music was loud and there were balloons tied everywhere.

'The first game is about to start! Come quick!' said Aditi, excitedly.

Penny ran along with her, patting her hair down. She noticed how her shoes shone, and how her skirt shimmered in the evening sunlight.

‘Ahoy, me hearties! There’s a wee bit of water on our boat,’ said Aditi’s mummy, with a twinkle in her eye, adjusting her pirate hat. ‘Your first game is to get the water off the boat. Two teams,’ she said, as she waved her arms across and away from each other, and divided the children. ‘And what you need to do, is to take the mug, fill it with water from here, run as fast as you can to the bucket there and empty it,’ she continued.

There was a roar of cheers from the children, and the game got underway.

Everyone ran as fast as they could, and the last person to get her team over the line was Penny. She ran fast, slipped on some spilt water … and fell down, flat on her face.

‘Are you okay, Penny?’ asked Aditi’s mummy.

'Yes,' she slowly replied. 'But my dress! My shoes! My hair!'

'Oh, don't worry, dear! We will clean you up, and you will be as good as new,' said Aditi's mummy.

Aditi's mummy took Penny inside the house. She scrubbed off the marks on her dress with some water and a brush. She wiped her shoes and patted down her hair. 'There! *Just* like you were before,' she said, with a smile on her face. 'Go on, now! Relax and have fun, Penny!'

Penny looked at herself in the mirror, in horror. Her dress had brown, blotchy marks on it. There was even a little rip at the side. Her shoes were wet and scuffed up. Her hair was standing up, tall as a coconut tree. There was even some mud and grass in her hair!

She joined the party, rather reluctantly.

The children had started on the next game. It was an art game, where they had to paint 'the boat'. 'The boat' was lots of newspapers stuck and draped over two chairs, in the shape of a boat.

'Penny! Here! Here!' yelled Aditi. 'We need you here. You are such a good artist. Can you tell us what colour you think we should use on this part in the front?'

Penny slowly walked towards Aditi, still worried about her dress. But pretty soon she was laughing hard and painting her side of the boat.

James reached over to rinse off his paintbrush in the jar filled with water and accidentally tipped the entire jar of dirty water into Penny's lap.

Penny looked down in shock. Her previously baby pink dress now looked green-orange-blue-grey-maroon-black-ish. It looked like a cat had been sick all over her perfect dress. Her shoes were soaked and squeaked as she stood up.

'Not your day, dear! But, don't worry, dear! We will clean you up and you will be as good as new,' said Aditi's mummy, keeping her tone neutral.

Aditi's mummy set to work, all over again. But this time, she was not as cheerful. 'It's okay, Penny. You can go home and take a shower, throw your dress in the washing machine, and you will be all good. Go on, now. Don't worry about how you look, just have fun!' she said, as she led her out.

The next game was already in progress. Aditi's daddy was the Captain of the ship, and he was shouting out orders ...

'Avast, crew! Here comes the Captain! Stand very still with your hands by your side!' 'Arrrrrr! Crew! Everybody, port side!'

Penny couldn't help herself. She thought she wouldn't play any more games, but she found herself joining in.

'Crew! All hands, on board! Time to scrub the deck! On your hands and knees, now!'

'Man overboard! Man overboard! Throw yourself down and drop your hand over to pull him up!'

Penny couldn't remember ever having more fun. She was lying on the ground, rolling around and laughing so much that her belly hurt.

‘Fire up the arms!’ yelled Penny’s daddy, and that meant that everyone had to sit on a balloon and hop on it over and over again, like a bunny, until it popped.

POP! Penny landed on her bottom with a thud!

‘Penny?’ she heard a voice call. ‘Is that really you? What happened here?’

She looked up and saw her mumma looking down at her, in utter disbelief.

Penny stopped smiling. She slowly stood up. She looked down at her shoes, she looked at her dress, her hand moved to her hair. She looked around at the mess on her and all around her. Then she saw Aditi waving to her and calling her over, as she was about to cut the cake.

Suddenly, she looked straight into her mumma's eyes and laughed and said, 'Yes! Yes, Mumma. It's really me. And this is fun too! Let's go eat some cake, Mumma!'

She bent down, picked up James' fallen eye patch, put it on her face and ran off to join Aditi.

6
Everyone Is Special

My friend Jai,
Can write real well,
He even knows,
How to spell.

But I can't.

My friend Pia,
Can throw a ball high,
It looks like a tiny plane,
Up in the sky.

But I can't.

My friend Aamir,
Can read already,
Every night,
To his big, brown teddy.

But I can't.

My friend Vibha,
Can run very fast,
She looks like a train,
Zooming past.

But I can't.

'I can't do any of this stuff,'
I pout,
But that's not what
It's all about.

Everyone can't be good
At everything,
But each of us is great
At something.

And if you don't know
What that is—don't fret,
It's not the right time,
For you to know it, yet.

Just try different things,
Have lots of fun,
Keep learning, keep trying,
You're never quite done.

Be patient too,
Try something new,
But above all,
Just be you.

There's just one,
ONLY one like you,
And you are special,
In what you do.

7

Neil's Homework

'Neil! You are going to be late!' Ma yelled. 'It's 8:58!'

Neil unhurriedly continued watching the YouTube video on his Papa's phone.

'Neil! Did you hear?' Ma yelled, even louder.

'Yes, Ma,' Neil replied.

Trrrrrrrrriiiiiiiinnnnnnnnnnnggggggggg!—The school bell loudly screamed out, precisely two minutes later.

As soon as Neil heard this, he ran to the chair, swung his school bag over his shoulder and sprinted out of his house screaming, 'Bye Ma! Bye Papa!' He didn't even have to wait for the lift, as he lived on the ground floor. He paused as he left his building gate, looked left, right, left again, then ran across the street, threw his school bag over the tall school wall, hoisted himself up onto the wall and slid down on the other side into ... guess where? Yes, right into the school compound.

You see, Neil thought he was the luckiest boy in the world. He lived right opposite his school.

This went on day after day. Neil's ma was fed up.

‘How long does it take to walk in from the gate, like all the other children in school, Neil?’ Ma asked.

‘True, but too boring, Ma. It’s faster over the wall,’ came Neil’s reply. ‘What’s the point of living opposite the school if I have to use the gate?’

‘That boy will never learn,’ Ma muttered to herself, shaking her head.

One morning, Neil walked into his class to find a new teacher there.

‘Good morning, children. I am your substitute Maths teacher, Mrs Andrade. I’m here to teach you Maths while Mrs Shah is on maternity leave. I have been teaching Maths for a long, long time. Way before you children were even born,’ said the new teacher, with a twinkle in her eye.

All the children looked at her, wide-eyed. She was so different from Mrs Shah. She was old and seemed really strict, just from her introduction. The children looked around at each other.

'Do you have any questions for me?' asked Mrs Andrade, in a loud voice.

Varun raised his hand.

'Yes?' asked Mrs Andrade, pointing out to him. 'But first, introduce yourself.'

'I'm Varun. And when will Mrs Shah be back?' questioned Varun.

'Mrs Shah actually had her baby early, Varun. The baby, a little girl, was born yesterday, early in the morning. She would have liked to have said goodbye to all of you herself, but since the baby came a bit early, she has to be home with her. She is on leave for three months. So, for the rest of this academic year I am your Maths teacher.'

Alia raised her hand.

'Yes! The young lady over there,' said Mrs Andrade, pointing to her.

'How old are you?' asked Alia.

Every child seemed to sit up straighter.

'First, please tell me your name, young lady,' said Mrs Andrade.

'Oh sorry. I forgot. I'm Alia,' she replied, with a small smile on her face.

‘Hello Alia. You must never ask a lady, her age, her weight or her income,’ Mrs Andrade replied, as she pushed her glasses up her nose with her long index fingernail. Then she smiled, and added, ‘However, I can say that I have retired. I have been a Maths teacher for over forty years. I have most certainly taught some of your parents. Maybe even some grandparents! Go home and ask them.’

Vivek raised his hand.

‘Yes?’ Mrs Andrade asked.

‘I am Vivek. Will you give us lots of homework?’

‘Great question, young man. Maths is all about practice. It’s like a muscle that needs to be exercised daily. That being said, I will not give you homework every day.’ She paused. She pushed her glasses up her nose again, with that long, pointy index fingernail.

Then she continued, 'I do have an interesting proposition for you all to consider, though. In the event that you do not do my homework, you will be off the hook IF—and only IF—you have an excuse that I have never heard before. Remember, children, I have been a Maths teacher for OVER FORTY years. I've heard a lot of excuses.'

Well, that's cool, thought Neil ... along with pretty much every child in the class.

The next few weeks were really quite uneventful. Mrs Andrade was strict, but she was fair. There was just one problem. The children just could not find an excuse that she hadn't heard of before, to get out of not doing homework. They had tried everything!

‘My dog ate my homework.’ (‘Seriously?’ asked Mrs Andrade. ‘Get more original, child.’)

‘I forgot.’ (‘Well that’s at least honest, but I’ve heard it before, Ravi,’ said Mrs Andrade.)

‘I did it, I really did, but I left it at home.’ (‘I’ve heard this excuse at least a million times, Gia,’ said Mrs Andrade.)

Neil was actually quite good at Maths; it was his favourite subject. His handwriting wasn’t very good, but his sums were almost always correct. Numbers made sense to him in a way that words didn’t. He found Maths easy.

On Monday morning, when Neil woke up, he saw that it was a dark and gloomy day. It was raining cats and dogs.

'Are you up?' Ma yelled from her bedroom. Neil dragged himself out of bed, and brushed his teeth. He had his bath, ate his breakfast and then took his Papa's phone to watch a YouTube video.

'Neil! You are going to be late!' Ma yelled. 'It's 8:58!'

Neil unhurriedly continued watching the YouTube video on his Papa's phone.

'Neil! Did you hear?' Ma yelled even louder.

'Yes, Ma,' Neil replied.

Trrrrrrrrriiiiiiiinnnnnnnnnnnggggggggg!—the school bell rang two minutes later.

'Take your raincoat!' Papa yelled, louder than the school bell.

Neil quickly buttoned on his raincoat, swung his school bag over his shoulder and sprinted out of his house screaming, 'Bye Ma! Bye Papa!'

As usual, he paused as he left his building gate, looked left, right, left again, then ran across the street, threw his school bag over the tall school wall, hoisted himself up onto the wall and slid down on the other side.

When he looked down to pick up his bag, he realized that his bag had fallen into a huge puddle and was completely soaked. But there was no time to think. He picked up his dripping wet bag and ran into class.

The first period was Maths, and Mrs Andrade said, 'Take out your homework and hand over your book to your neighbour for corrections.'

Neil was fumbling in his wet bag. All his books were soaked. Neil wondered what he could do.

Before he could say anything, Mrs Andrade said, 'A-ha! We seem to have a problem here. What's your excuse, Neil?'

Neil stood up. He looked her in the eye and said, 'I did my homework. Really. But here's what happened. I live just opposite school. So, I don't use the gate. I throw my bag over the wall into the school compound, and then jump over the wall. I forgot it was raining, and when I threw my bag over, it landed in a big puddle. It stayed in that puddle till I jumped over. My bag is soaked—my book is dripping wet, and the pages are all wet. And I wrote my homework with a pencil ...'

There was complete silence.

And then Mrs Andrade's face lit up. She smiled a smile the children had never seen before and said, 'Congratulations, Neil! You have a green pass for not doing your homework. I have never heard that excuse before, in over forty years of teaching!'

8

Anne

We have a cat,
A naughty cat,
He's cute and fuzzy,
But acts like a brat.

He loves to play,
He loves to sleep,
He loves to eat,
He loves to leap.

But most of all,
Our naughty cat,
Loves to play with the ants,
On our mat.

Now busy worker ants,
Do not like to be disturbed,
By cats, dogs or even plants,
But our cat is unperturbed.

The sad part is,
Our cat has pointy claws,
He hurts the ants,
With his paws.

The ants got angry,
'That cat's a pest,
He knows he is bigger,
But just won't give it a rest.'

Once the Queen Ant heard of it,
She called for a meeting,
'So we know the problem,
How can we stop this mistreating?'

'But what can we do?'
'We are just too small!'
'How can we win,
Against that cat in a brawl?'

The Queen Ant replied,
'We are small in size, that's true,
But let's think about our strengths,
There are quite a few.'

'For starters,
We can run very fast,
And in number,
Few can go past.'

'We can lift things heavier
than our own weight,
We need a real plan,
And to not leave this to fate.'

Everyone was thinking,
There was a quiet hush in the meeting,
Then suddenly ...
There was a movement in the seating.

It was the tiniest ant,
Littlest Anne,
Attending her first big meeting,
Who had a plan.

The next day,
Out ran our cat,
He spotted the ants,
And went straight to the mat.

The ants saw him coming,
They got together and huddled,
Our cat stopped and stared,
He was quite befuddled.

Then quick as can be,
The ants formed a tall tower,
Each one concentrating,
On their joint superpower.

Each ant found his place,
On the back of an ant,
Only slightly bigger than himself,
And no ant said, 'I can't.'

Every ant found his spot,
His very own space,
And as one tall creature,
They stared our cat in the face.

Our cat looked scared,
He just could not move,
He froze to inaction,
These ants had something to prove.

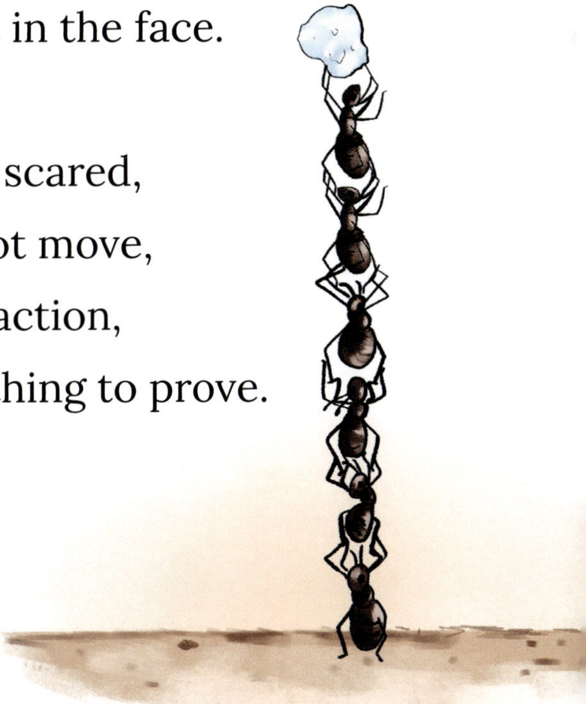

Together, they were tall,
Together, they were strong,
Together, they were fearless,
No one could do them wrong.

They were as tall as our cat,
And they did not run,
They stood their ground,
They knew this HAD to be done.

Then littlest Anne,
At the very top of the line,
Looked towards our cat,
Her face seemed to shine.

She looked him steady,
Straight in his eye,
And loudly demanded,
'Why cat, WHY?'

And fast as a flash,
Our cat made a dash.

As fast as he could,
Away from the ants ...
Like they KNEW he would.

And the Queen Ant said, 'Ah, good!'

We have a cat,
A naughty cat,
He still loves to play,
But after that day,

He keeps away,
Far away, from the ants.

9

As Busy as a Bee

Neeraj was bored. As bored as can be. He was stuck indoors, as it was raining buckets outside. He needed something to do on this dull, dark, grey, gloomy day.

'Nothing ever happens! It's so boooorrrring!' he cried out, stomping his foot and sticking his lower lip out.

His mummy was busy. As busy as a bee.

She said, 'Oh Neeraj! I'm so busy! I have one hundred things that need to get done, as of yesterday. But I have an idea! Why don't you draw something?'

So, Neeraj took a paper and pencil and drew a castle, then a frog, then some clouds, then a sun, then a monster. Then he got bored and scribbled all over it.

'Nothing ever happens! It's so boooorrrring!' he cried out, stomping his foot and sticking his lower lip out.

His mummy was busy. As busy as a bee.

She said, 'Oh Neeraj! I'm so busy! I have seventy-five things that need to get done, as of yesterday. But I have an idea! Why don't you look at the pictures in the books that we borrowed from the library yesterday?'

So, Neeraj went to his bedroom, pulled out his library bag from the drawer, and took out the picture books they had borrowed. He opened the first book and looked at the pictures, he opened the next book and looked at the pictures. Then he got bored and shut it with a snaaaaaaaap!

'Nothing ever happens! It's so boooorrrring!' he cried out, stomping his foot and sticking his lower lip out.

His mummy was busy. As busy as a bee.

She said, 'Oh Neeraj! I'm so busy! I have fifty things that need to get done, as of yesterday. But I have an idea! Why don't you figure out a jigsaw puzzle?'

So, Neeraj went to the cupboard and picked out a jigsaw puzzle. He pulled the pieces out the box and turned them over. One piece slipped under the bed. He tried to crawl under to get it. But he could not fit. Then he went to his room, got a bat and swooshed the piece out from under the bed. He started by doing the corners. He joined three pieces, then four more, then two more pieces together. Then he got bored, and kicked the pieces around. He made sure a few went under the bed.

'Nothing ever happens! It's so boooorrrring!' he cried out, stomping his foot and sticking his lower lip out.

His mummy was busy. As busy as a bee.

She said, 'Oh Neeraj! I'm so busy! I have twenty-five things that need to get done, as of yesterday.

But I have a brilliant idea! Why don't you play with your blocks?'

So, Neeraj went over to the shelf to find his building blocks.

But they weren't there. He looked high and low for them. When he opened the drawers in the toy cupboard, his eyes fell on a new box of tattoo crayons that his grandma had given him for his birthday. The words **LOOKS PERFECTLY REAL ON SKIN** were boldly printed on the box.

He took them out, just to have a look. He tried drawing a monster tattoo on his leg. It looked perfect. He'd seen people on TV who had tattoos on their entire arms, legs ... so he drew some more. First on his other leg. Then on his arms. He found the right colours and even coloured them in.

When his body was fully covered with them, his eye fell on the wall. 'It looks so bare,' he murmured to himself.

So, he took the crayons over to the wall. He tilted his head to the left, and whispered, 'Maybe just one sun and some trees?'

A whole forest later, he heard his mummy say, 'Neeraj! Neeraj! Where are you? I've finished all my work, there's nothing more left to do. Now I can play with you.'

Neeraj heard footsteps. His mummy was soon at the door. Then she was in the room.

'NEERAJ!' she screeched. 'What have you done?'

'But I was soooo bored and you were as busy as

a bee,' Neeraj whined, stomping his foot just a teeny tiny bit, and sticking his lower lip out, as tears filled his eyes.

'And it's a forest, and I'm a monster hiding in the forest, and … and … and … ' Neeraj burst into huge, loud sobs.

'Ah!' said his mummy. 'Why didn't you say that? Now I see it! Why don't we lose the monster and make him a boy again? I have a special spell for that right here in our bathroom.'

She pulled him into her arms, and waved her hands over him and uttered in a creaky, shaky tone,
'Igitty-bigitty,
Bring me some joy,
Take away this monster,
Bring me a boy!'

And then she took him to the bathroom and scrubbed him down. As big soap bubbles floated around, she said, 'Ah perfect! No monster in sight, just my little boy Neeraj again.'

Then she picked up a bucket and a sponge. She held Neeraj's hand and said, 'Now we need another spell to remove some trees from the forest, so that we can sleep at night without being afraid of the wild animals roaming in it.'

She waved her hands over the wall and uttered in a creaky, shaky tone,
'Igitty-bigitty,
We need a room,
Take away this forest,
With all its gloom!'

Then she scrubbed down the wall (all except two

trees). When she was done, she lay down on the bed and said, 'Ah perfect! No forest in sight, just two trees in my boy's room.'

She sighed, and pulled Neeraj down next to her.

Neeraj was all smiles. He lay down beside his mummy, and swung his leg across her tummy.

Then suddenly he sat up, looked around him. 'Nothing ever happens! It's so boooorrrring!' he cried out, stomping his foot on the mattress, and sticking his lower lip out.

Luckily, it was time for bed.

'Goodnight, Neeraj,' sighed his mummy.

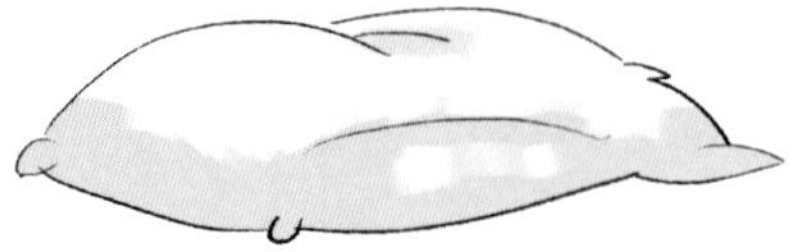

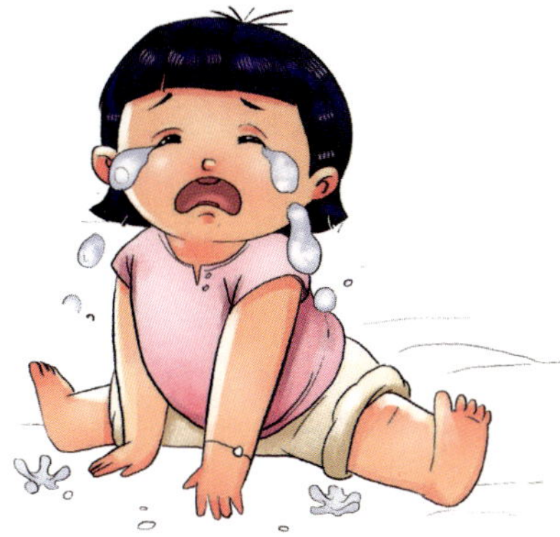

10

Jennifer's Boys

We were at the beach,
My mummy, my daddy and I,
It was lots of fun,
The sun shone in the sky.

Who should come beside us?
Two very active boys,
With plastic swords and shovels,
Amongst their other toys.

I looked up at their mummy,
She smiled down at me,
I didn't smile back at her,
I looked right at the sea.

My daddy said, 'Hello',
And then they started chatting,
My mummy smiled at theirs,
And I started babbling.

'This here is our Jennifer,
She's not quite speaking yet,'
said Mummy with a wink.
'But she'll get there soon, I bet.'

'Say hello, Jennifer!
Say hi, sweet child,'
Mummy tried cajoling,
But Daddy only smiled.

'Are they frightening you, Jennifer?'
The boys' mummy asked me,
I didn't look back at her,
I looked right at the sea.

I peeked at the boys,
They were having lots of fun,
'Would you like to join them, Jenny?'
I looked up at the sun.

They started building castles,
Sand flying here and there,
Some of it even landed,
On my brand-new teddy bear.

The boys' mummy came over,
She cleaned up Teddy and said,
'Easy boys, be careful!'
She smiled and shook her head.

They laughed and yelled out,
'Mummy! Come see! Come!
Bring Jenny too, Mummy!'
I looked down at a crumb.

They started playing football,
With a big and bouncy ball,
It rolled fast and to stop it,
One boy had a fall.

The boys' daddy ran over,
He picked him up and said,
'Easy boys, be careful!'
He smiled and shook his head.

They laughed and shouted loudly,
'Daddy! Come play in the sand!'
'Would you like to play too, Jenny?'
I stared down at my hand.

They started running from the waves,
Laughing loudly, running fast,
One wave caught one boy,
And splashed him and went past.

The boys' mummy went over,
She hugged him tight and said,
'Easy boys, be careful!'
She smiled and shook her head.

They laughed and shouted loudly,
'Come catch waves Mummy, come try!'
'Would you like to catch waves, Jenny?'
I looked up at the sky.

It was now getting dark,
The boys' mummy called them back,
'It's time to get you cleaned up,
And to bathe, before a snack!'

I saw the boys run up,
I saw the boys get dry,
I saw the boys put on their shoes,
And then I started to cry.

'What's up, baby Jenny?'
'What happened, sweet pea?'
'Are you tired? Are you hungry?'
'Enough of the big, blue sea?'

I cried and cried and cried,
I made lots of tears and noise,
And then ... just like that I said,
My very first word—'Boys.'

11

Mr Moon

‘Bye-bye, Nani! Bye-bye, Nana,’ said Arjun.

‘We need to find an auto rickshaw first, Arju,’ said Mumma, holding his hand tight, and leading him towards the front door.

‘Aren’t we forgetting something?’ asked Papa.

Arjun looked at Papa, tilted his head to one side, shook his head vigorously and said, ‘I know what you are asking, Papa. No, I don't need to use the toilet before we leave.'

'Are you sure?' asked Mumma, giving his hand a little squeeze. 'Go, try,' she coaxed. 'It's at least forty-five minutes in the auto rickshaw, till we reach home.'

Arjun ran off to the toilet, and Nana followed him. When he came out, Nana asked, 'When will you come to see us again, Arju? Next Sunday?'

'Next Sunday, Nana,' Arjun replied. Nana bent down and gave him a hug.

They all walked down the road to try to flag down an empty auto rickshaw. 'They don't come to this side easily anymore, as they've now made this road a one way,' Nani grumbled.

‘Let’s walk to the junction,’ Nana said, pointing ahead, and leading the way.

As they stood by the side of the road, they saw cars and bikes zoom by, but there wasn’t an empty rickshaw in sight. Till suddenly, Papa spotted one. *Pheeeeeeeeoooo-pee*, Nana whistled. Arjun turned and looked at Nana in admiration, then looked back to see if the auto rickshaw driver had heard. How could he have not? The driver seemed to pause, then he turned the auto rickshaw sharply and was now speeding towards them.

Nani was already hugging Mumma and Arjun. ‘Will you teach me to whistle like that, Nana?’ Arjun whispered in Nana’s ear, as he hugged him.

‘Of course,’ Nana’s moustache tickled Arjun’s ear. Arjun couldn’t stop smiling.

And then, Arjun, Mumma and Papa were in the auto rickshaw, and on their way home. Arjun was sitting in the middle and his Mumma and Papa were on either side of him. As the auto rickshaw sped forward, the fresh breeze ruffled his hair. It was nice and cool. Arjun moved his head towards it.

Arjun bent down and looked through the windshield, and saw a big cow in the middle of the road. The auto rickshaw slowed down a little, then as they passed the cow, Arjun saw that she was, not in front of him, but to his left. And then they drove past her. Arjun looked behind, and gave the cow a little wave. She was now behind them. As he watched her, she grew smaller and smaller, till he couldn't see her anymore.

Arjun glanced towards his left again. Something else caught his eye. It was the crescent Mr Moon, smiling down on him, between two buildings. He smiled back at him.

He immediately sang the words of a nursery rhyme his Mumma sang to him each night.

'There, right there,
Up in the sky,
Is Mr Moon,
Way up high.

His shape is crescent,
Like a smile,
You can see him shine,
From a mile.'

A while later, Arjun bent down and looked through the windshield again, and saw a red double-decker bus in front of them. The auto rickshaw sped up, then as they passed the bus, Arjun saw that it was, not in front of him, but to his left. And then they drove past it. Arjun looked behind, and gave the bus a little wave. It was now behind them. As he watched it, it grew smaller and smaller, till he couldn't see it anymore.

Arjun glanced towards his left again. The bus had gone, but the crescent moon was still there. He was STILL smiling down on him. Arjun smiled back at him.

He again sang the words of a nursery rhyme his Mumma sang to him each night.

'There, right there,
Up in the sky,
Is Mr Moon,
Way up high.

His shape is crescent,
Like a smile,
You can see him shine,
From a mile.'

After some time, Arjun bent down and looked through the windshield again, and saw his favourite toy shop 'Teeny-Meny' in front of them. The auto rickshaw sped up, then as they passed the shop, Arjun saw that it was, not in front of him, but to his left. He even saw the shop uncle sitting at the counter in the shop. Then they drove past it. Arjun looked behind, and gave the shop a little wave. It was now behind them. As he watched it, it grew smaller and smaller, till he couldn't see it anymore.

Arjun glanced towards his left again. They had gone past the shop, but the crescent moon was still there. He was STILL smiling down on him. Arjun gave the moon a wave, and he smiled a big smile back at him.

He once again sang the words of a nursery rhyme his Mumma sang to him each night.

'There, right there,
Up in the sky,
Is Mr Moon,
Way up high.

His shape is crescent,
Like a smile,
You can see him shine,
From a mile.'

The auto rickshaw slowed down to a stop, as they reached home. While Papa paid the driver, Arjun pulled at Mumma's hand to go home. He was tired.

He stepped out when the elevator doors opened, and waited impatiently as Papa opened the front door. As Arjun walked into the living room, his eye fell on something. He blinked with surprise. He couldn't believe it! He ran to the window of the living room and looked outside, in delight.

'Mumma! Papa!' Arjun yelled, pointing. 'Look! Look! It's Mr Moon! He followed us home. I saw him when we were in the auto rickshaw. He followed us all the way from Nana and Nani's home, and right to our home. I think he likes me.'

'Oh Arju!' Papa laughed. 'It only seems that way, because Mr Moon is so very far away from us. He didn't really follow us home. But you are right about one thing. He DOES like you. See his shape? Crescent. Just like your smile.'

12

Smile

My mum always says,
'Smile and say hello.'
Even to people
I don't really know.

She says, 'A smile
Can change someone's day.
It helps to make
Their pain go away.'

She says, 'A smile
Makes it all worthwhile,
It helps people go
That extra mile.'

She says, 'A smile's
The opposite of a frown,
And makes you feel
Like you're wearing a crown.'

I think my mum's right,
When I'm with a smile on,
My world shines brighter,
And my problems are gone.

When I smile,
My eyes sparkle with light,
Like twinkling stars
On a dull, dark night.

With a smile on my face,
I look real friendly,
And with one on,
I'm hip and trendy.

So if you want
To look your very best,
Go on, try it,
Give it a test.

Wake up each morning
With a smile,
Then smile again
After a while.

It's noon time now,
What must you do?
Smile of course,
There's your clue.

Evening's here,
Time for something new,
Smile and say,
'So nice to see you.'

When darkness falls,
And Mr Moon's up high,
Smile and wish
The day goodbye.

So remember to smile
From morning to night,
A smile makes everything
Feel just right.

13

Ria's Pets

Ria loved animals. Any animal. All animals. She didn't really have a preference. She could spend hours just watching them. They were so interesting, and each one was so special. While waiting for the school bus, she would make friends with the street dogs, the cats and even the birds. She could watch them for hours. Sometimes she was so busy watching the birds that she didn't notice that the school bus had arrived till someone nudged her.

While helping Ma in the kitchen, Ria noticed the ants walking in a line, up the kitchen wall. One behind the other. No one was telling them how to walk, but they did it.

'How can ants walk in a straight line without even using a ruler, Ma? Do they even know that it is straight?' she asked.

'Hmmm. I'm not sure, Ria,' Ma replied. 'Maybe we should Google it.'

And that was that for Ma. But not for Ria. She continued watching them hurriedly walking in a line, going upwards and then turning right, once again in a straight line, now walking towards the window. Not one second to spare, not one pause in the line. They seemed so busy. Ria found it fascinating.

While sitting with Papa in the balcony, she watched the bees buzzing around their hive, which was hanging from a tree branch. Round and round they went, not pausing for even a second.

'Do bees get giddy, Papa? I mean as they fly around and around?' she asked.

'Hmmm ... I'm not sure, Ria,' her papa replied. 'Maybe we should Google it.'

And that was that for Papa. But not for Ria. She continued watching them busily flying around in a circle, their wings catching the light as they flew. Ria found them fascinating.

While doing her homework, she heard the crows talking to each other. She left the table and went to her window.

‘Caw! Caw! Caw! Caw!’ they said to each other. A bunch of them were sitting on the wires, connected to the street light poles. *Are they having a party*? Ria wondered.

Then suddenly, when she looked to the right, she heard the pigeons on the air conditioner’s big rectangular box outside the window.

‘Coo! Coo! Coo! Coo!’ they went.

‘Do the pigeons understand the crows, Ma? Are coos and caws the same in bird language?’ she asked, curiously.

‘Hmmm. I’m not sure, Ria,’ Ma replied. ‘Maybe we should Google it.’

And that was that for Ma. But not for Ria.

Coo
Coo
Coo
Coo

CAW
CAW
CAW
CAW
CAW
CAW
CAW

She continued watching the crows. *Maybe it is a meeting, not a party*, she thought. *Maybe they are angry, not happy. That's why they are being* so *very loud.*

She longed for a pet of her own.

'Can we have a dog please, Ma?' she asked.

'When you are a little older,' Ma replied.

'But why? How old must I be?' she whined. 'I'm old enough NOW!'

'Not quite,' Ma replied, shaking her head. And that was that for Ma.

'Can we have a cat please, Papa?' she asked. 'Please? I'll do everything for it!'

‘Soon, Ria,’ Papa replied.

‘But when?’ she whined. ‘When is soon? In a week? Why not now?’

‘In a while,’ Papa replied, shaking his head. And that was that for Papa.

Nana saw Ria’s face fall. Nani saw her rapidly blink back tears.

Nana and Nani’s eyes met over Ria’s head. Nana gave a slight nod.

‘Psst!’ said Nani.

Ria looked up.

‘Look what I have for you, Ria!’ Nani said,

bringing out something large and heavy from her room. She needed both hands to carry it.

Ria paused. Her eyes widened.

She grabbed it out of Nani's hands. It had the words ***ENCYCLOPEDIA OF ANIMALS*** printed in big on the cover. Ria excitedly turned the glossy pages.

For now, Ria had a book full of pets.

14

Hurricane Boy

My mum calls me a hurricane,
I often ask her why,
She says, 'It's only because I love you,
From the ground up to the sky.'

I'm not too sure about that,
I think I might know why …
I somehow seem to tap things,
As I'm quickly going by.

I know I run real fast,
I need my arms to move,
It's what all us runners do,
It helps our speed improve.

I run to get a book,
I go over as fast as I can,
Suddenly the vase tips over,
It wasn't part of the plan.

I know I'm great at football,
I've got a super duper kick,
It's what all us footballers have,
To pass and shoot real quick.

I give the ball a mighty kick,
It rolls towards the wall,
It hits the coffee table,
And things begin to fall.

I know I'm fast on my scooter,
I've got a strong, powerful push,
It's what all us scooty boys have,
It helps the air go, 'Whooosh!'

I love my lime green scooter,
There's nothing like it to zoom,
Who keeps cups on a table?
Oops! CRASH-BOOM!

I know I'm great at climbing,
I've got muscles in each arm,
It's what all us climbers have,
It keeps us safe from harm.

Our cookie jar's high on a shelf,
Just perfect for climbers like me,
It's not my fault when it slides off,
I hope you will agree.

I'm five and a big boy now,
I can do everything all alone,
It's what us big boys do,
A fact that's so well-known.

I love to do things by myself,
Like pour juice into my cup,
But the box gets wet and sweaty,
And slips as I stand up.

I walk into the kitchen,
I'm looking for the mop,
I don't want mum to see the juice,
I know she'll lose her top.

There's mum looking grumpy,
She's on her knees with a broom,
She sits down when she sees me,
But I can still see her fume.

‘I spilt the bag of raw rice,
It’s all over the floor,
Rolled down from the counter,
And right up to the door.’

I laugh and laugh and laugh,
I think I could laugh all day,
I finally stop for a minute,
And chortle out and say …

‘Mum, you’re a hurricane too,
And I will tell you why,
It’s only because I love you,
From the ground up to the sky.’

15

Dad's Big, Black Office Shoes

There's a tradition in my family. One that I love. Every Sunday morning, right about nine, Dad brings out his big, black office shoes.

My dad's really big. He is six feet tall. And his shoes are HUGE! Both my feet can fit inside just one of his shoes. It's true!

My sister and I wait for precisely that moment,

because we get to be his chief helpers. It's the best part of our Sunday. I run to bring the shoe polish, and Mira runs to bring the newspaper. Bolt, our cat, just runs. I think he's a little afraid that we might run over him, so he just runs out of the way.

My dad, my sister and I,
Polishing away, making Dad's shoes shine,
Every Sunday morning,
Right about nine.

It's a tradition, and I love it.

First we have to spread out the newspapers flat and overlapping, as Ma hates it when the polish leaves marks on the floor.

Then my dad opens the shoe polish box.

We each get to put a dab of it on his big, black office shoes. Mira gets Dad's left shoe and I get his right one.

My dad gives each of us a brush, and now comes the tough part. We both have to brush and brush and brush. I feel like my arm will fall off.

Then we swap shoes, and brush again. Brush and brush and brush. Phew!

'Put some muscle into it and brush till they shine, girls!' encourages my dad.

My dad, my sister and I,
Polishing away, making Dad's shoes shine,
Every Sunday morning,
Right about nine.

It's a tradition, and I love it.

Last Sunday, some of that polish smell got inside Mira's nose and tickled it. She sneezed just as she was brushing Dad's shoe, and she got black shoe polish on her nose. We laughed and laughed and Mira didn't know why. So we had to pause the polishing, and take her to the mirror, before she started crying. Little sisters do that a lot. They cry.

Mira STILL didn't think it was funny, so Dad put some polish on his nose as well, and of course then my nose needed some too. Bolt rubbed himself on Dad's legs as we goofed around. He didn't think it was funny. His nose is pink.

After all the laughing about our noses, we had to get back to work, back to the polishing, of course.

My dad, my sister and I,
Polishing away, making Dad's shoes shine,
Every Sunday morning,
Right about nine.

It's a tradition, and I love it.

My dad says, 'You should never grow too big to polish your own shoes.'

Then he takes his newly-polished shoes and keeps them out in the sun to dry. My dad says a lot of stuff. But this is one of the things I will always remember.

When I'm all grown up, I hope to get an office job, just like my dad. I can wear long trousers, long-sleeved shirts, a fancy scarf around my neck, and big, black office shoes—just like my dad.

And every Sunday morning, right about nine, my children and I will bring out the polish box, spread out the newspapers, dab the polish on and brush and brush till MY big, black office shoes shine!

MY children and I,
Polishing away, making MY shoes shine,
Every Sunday morning,
Right about nine.

A tradition moving forward, and I love it.

If I listen really carefully, as I keep my newly-polished shoes in the sun to dry, I can hear myself saying to my children, 'You should never grow too big to polish your own shoes.'

16

I Love Dinosaurs

I love to play,
I love all my toys,
Some are silent,
Some make a noise.

Some have wheels,
Others have paws,
But the ones I love most,
Are my dinosaurs.

'Where are your dolls?'
People often ask me,
I bring out my dinos,
... Happily.

Dinosaurs are cool,
Dinosaurs are fun,
Dinos look awesome,
When they run.

Some are huge,
Others are tiny,
Some are dull-coloured,
Others are shiny.

Some are silent,
Others have a cry,
Some can swim,
Others can fly.

Some look friendly,
Others look scary,
Some are feathered,
Others are hairy.

Some walk on two,
Others on four feet,
Some eat greens,
Others eat only meat.

Some have long necks,
Others have huge heads,
Some have pointy horns,
That everyone dreads.

Some run fast,
Some are slow,
But there's always a thud,
On the ground below.

The one thing that's common
To almost all,
Is their tongue twisting names,
That are hard to call.

The thing that's interesting
about their names,
Is that they have meanings,
I'm not making tall claims.

Here are just a few,
To prove my case,
Try saying them aloud,
With a straight face.

There's Apatosaurus—Deceptive lizard,
And Brachiosaurus—Arm lizard,
Spinosaurus—Thorn lizard
And Gigantosaurus—Gigantic lizard.

Now meet, Dilophosaurus—Two crested lizard,
And Stegosaurus—Roofed lizard.
(Don't they sound like a mouthful of spells,
From a world-famous wizard?)

Flat like a plate,
Is Plateosaurus,
While the one that's bent,
Is Ankylosaurus.

I could go on and on
and add to the list,
But the two that
just can't be missed are ...

Triceratops,
With its three horned face,
And Tyrannosaurus Rex,
The king of the race.

I love dinosaurs,
They are so much fun,
Though extinct, they're awesome,
I love each one.

17
The Hiccups

Hic!

Hic!

Hic!

Aarav looked up, surprised. They seemed to come from his tummy, but his entire body jerked each time they rose out of his mouth.

Hic!

Hic!

He had the hiccups.

Hic!

Hic!

Hic!

His body shook from his belly button, to the hair on his head. And it felt a little tickly.

'Maaaaaaa-ic!' he yelled out.

'What is it, Aarav?' his ma replied.

'Hic!' said Aarav, though he didn't exactly plan on saying that.

'Ah! You have the hics. Drink some water, Aarav,' said Ma and went back to watering her plants on the balcony.

Aarav drank a big glass of water. He put the glass down, sure that this would be the end of the hics. He waited for a few seconds, started to smile with relief, when ...

Hic!

Hic!

Hic!

Hic!

'Daaaaadddyy-ic!' he yelled out.

'What is it, Aarav?' his daddy replied.

'Hic!' said Aarav. He knew he'd say it, but he still looked surprised when he did.

'Ah! You have the hics. You need a spoonful of sugar,' said Daddy, handing him the sugar jar, and then going back to stirring the dinner that was bubbling on the stove.

'Yum!' said Aarav, with a big smile. He loved sugar. He put the spoon down. He waited a few seconds, started to smile with relief, when ...

Hic!
Hic!
Hic!

'Ranvirrrrrr-ic!' he yelled out.

'What is it, Aarav?' Ranvir replied.

'Hic!' said Aarav. He wasn't even surprised anymore.

'Ah! You have the hics. We need to tickle you. There is no other way to stop them,' said Ranvir.

Tickle-tickle-tickle.

HA-HA-HA!

Hic!

Hic!

Hic!

Tickle-tickle-tickle.

Hee-Hee-Hee!

Hic!

Hic!

Hic!

Hic!

CRASH!

‘What happened, Aarav?’ Daddy asked, running towards Aarav and Ranvir.

‘Oh no!’ said Ma, dramatically putting her hand to her head. ‘What have you boys done, now?’

While Ranvir was tickling Aarav, he kicked the big bowl of fruit that Ma had kept on the coffee table.

Apples spun here.

Oranges bounced there.

Grapes rolled everywhere.

Aarav and Ranvir got down on their knees, and helped Ma and Daddy pick up the fruit. Ranvir squashed two grapes under his knees and made a bigger mess. Daddy accidentally stepped on the

mushy mess, making everything so much worse than it was!

Ma angrily shouted, 'Go and get the mop, Ranvir!'

As he stood to get it, Aarav laughed.

'Ranvir, guess what? I think we scared my hiccups away!' he said.

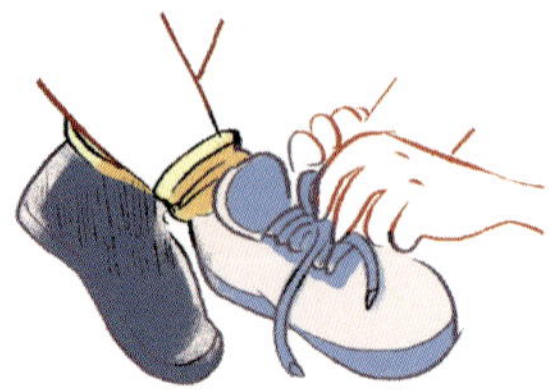

18
The Best Deed

I helped an old lady,
Cross the street,
Walking that slow,
Was quite a feat.

Is that a good deed?

I helped my little brother,
Tie his shoe lace,
I tied it up double,
Just in case.

Is that a good deed?

I told my teacher,
She looked pretty,
She looked like the happiest,
Girl in the city.

Is that a good deed?

I planted a small tree,
In my garden today,
It makes the world greener,
And cleaner they say.

Is that a good deed?

I drew a card,
For my best friend at school,
He saw it and loved it,
And said it was cool.

Is that a good deed?

All these are good deeds,
I should make clear,
If you've done any of these,
You've nothing to fear.

'But what's the best deed?'
You might ask,
Listen carefully,
It's not a tough task.

The best deed ...
The one that's most swell,
It's simple really,
Just DO and DON'T TELL.

19
Diamonds in the Sky

As Alia and Papa lay down in her bed, she happened to look at the sky through the grills on her window.

Twinkle!
Twinkle!
Twinkle!
The stars winked down at her.

'Papa! Look!' Alia whispered, pointing towards the window and to the sky.

‘Yes,’ said Papa. ‘Aren’t they beautiful? Stars always remind me of diamonds sparkling in the night sky.’

‘How can I catch one, Papa?’ Alia asked.

‘Well, they are really far away. What do you think we can do to catch one?’ asked Papa, his eyes twinkling almost as much as the stars.

‘I know!’ Alia replied, jumping out of bed. ‘Come, Papa, come!’

She held Papa’s hand and dragged him out of the front door, into the garden.

And then, she jumped. She jumped and jumped and jumped. She stretched her hands high up in the air, as she jumped. Tired of trying, she sat on the grass and looked up to the sky.

'They really are up so high,
Way up there in the sky,'
Alia said, in wonder.

Twinkle!
Twinkle!
Twinkle!
The stars winked down at her.

The next night, Alia had a plan.

As soon as it was bedtime, she dragged Papa out in the garden once more. She kept him waiting there, and ran back inside.

'Where are you going, Alia?' Papa asked.

'I'll be back in a minute!' she replied with a huge smile on her face.

True to her word, she was back in a minute. But this time, with her pogo stick.

And then she hopped. She hopped and hopped and hopped. She hopped higher on her pogo stick, than she had just by herself. But she still wasn't quite high enough. Tired of trying, she sat on the grass and looked up to the sky.

'They really are up so high,
Way up there in the sky,'
Alia said, in wonder.

Twinkle!
Twinkle!
Twinkle!
The stars winked down at her.

The following night, Alia tried again.

As soon as it was bedtime, she dragged Papa out in the garden once more. She pulled him further into the garden, till they reached the mango tree.

‘Hmmm,’ said Papa.

‘I’ll climb it, Papa!’ she replied. ‘Look how high the branches are. They are touching the sky!’

Up and up she went.

‘Be careful,’ Papa yelled.

‘I’ve done this so often, Papa,’ Alia replied. ‘Just that I normally climb it in the daytime.’

Alia reached the highest branch. She paused to catch her balance and stretched her arms up to grab a star.

But she wasn't quite high enough. Tired of trying, she climbed back down. She sat on the grass and looked up to the sky.

'They really are up so high,
Way up there in the sky,'
Alia said, in wonder, and just a bit of anger.

Twinkle!
Twinkle!
Twinkle!
The stars winked down at her.

The next night, Alia tried again.

As soon as it was bedtime, she dragged Papa out in the garden once more.

'Wait here for me, Papa. I will be back soon,'

she said, with a quick wave as she ran towards the kitchen.

She came back with Usha didi, who was carrying Mumma's ladder from the kitchen. Usha didi leant the ladder against the wall, and up went Alia.

Papa smiled as he watched her go. Step by step, she went higher and higher.

Alia reached the highest rung of the ladder. She stretched her arms up to grab a star. But she wasn't quite high enough.

She tried on tippy toes, and really stretched. But she STILL just wasn't high enough.

She climbed back down, feeling a little bit sad. She sat on the grass and looked up to the sky.

‘They really are up so high,
Way up there in the sky,’
Alia said, in wonder, and with a touch of sadness.

Twinkle!
Twinkle!
Twinkle!
The stars winked down at her.

The following night, Alia tried—yet again.

As soon as it was bedtime, she dragged Papa out in the garden once more.

Then she brought out a kite. Keeping her back to the wind, exactly how Papa had taught her, she jumped, and let it go. But there just wasn’t enough wind to catch the kite and lift it up into the sky. Alia tried and tried.

Each time she got more and more disappointed.

Finally, she sat on the grass and looked up to the sky. 'I thought the kite would hook onto a star, and bring it down to me.'

'It was worth a try, Alia,' said Papa.

'They really are up so high,
Way up there in the sky,'
Alia said, with frustration.

Twinkle!
Twinkle!
Twinkle!
The stars winked down at her.

The next morning, when Alia woke up, Papa had a surprise for her. He had a big bucket of black paint.

Papa rolled in the ladder.

While Alia held the bucket up, Papa dipped into it and together they painted the ceiling of her room black.

'Why are we doing this, Papa?' Alia asked, over and over again.

'You'll see,' Papa replied, over and over again.

'It's going to take all day for the paint to dry,' said Papa, once they were done. 'So, let's go outside to play today.'

That evening, as the sun went down, and as the sky grew dim, Papa held Alia's hand and led her into her bedroom. He made her sit on the bed, as he pulled the curtains shut.

Then in the pitch darkness of the room, he lay on her bed, and pulled her to lie down next to him. Before he could say a word, Alia said one. Just one.

'Wow!'

Blinking down on Alia, from the black painted ceiling of her bedroom, were stars. Her Papa had stuck them on the ceiling, just for her.

'Stars must stay in the sky, Alia. You can't catch them in your hands,' said Papa, pulling her close.

'I think that's what makes them look just like diamonds sparkling in the night sky, Papa,' she replied.

20

My Undies

Right after a bath,
When I'm squeaky clean and bare,
I love to go to my closet,
And choose my underwear.

My mum doesn't understand,
Just ask her, and she'll admit,
'It shouldn't take so much time,
Just pick the ones that fit.'

But it's so much more than the fit,
They need to be 'just right',
They need to go with what I'm doing,
Even though they're out of sight.

I only use the dino ones,
When I go to the zoo,
I can't have dinos in my pants,
When helping Dad cook stew.

I only use the race car ones,
When I'm zipping on my bike,
I can't have race cars in my pants,
When I'm singing on a mic.

I only use the airplane ones,
When we travel on a holiday,
I can't have airplanes in my pants,
To roll out snakes in clay.

I only use the stripey ones,
On days we eat spaghetti,
I can't have stripes in my pants,
To play football and get sweaty.

I only use the pirate ones,
On days we play in the sand,
I can't have pirates in my pants,
With crayons in my hand.

I only use the grey ones,
When it's gloomy, dull and rainy,
I can't have grey in my pants,
To do homework and be brainy.

So you see, I need the right ones,
It depends on the plan for the day,
It's not as easy as my mum thinks,
... Much to her dismay.

21

Bertha's Spot

Everyone on the river knows Bertha's spot. She sits, as still as a statue, sunning herself every day. She sits with her eyes closed; she doesn't move a muscle. She doesn't flinch, even when it is windy.

Kenny, the crab, clambers over Mummy, crawls up a rock and then climbs onto the sticky mud on the riverbank. The first thing he sees is big Bertha, the crocodile. He quickly takes a step back.

Mummy notices this. 'Oh Ken,' she says, 'That's Bertha's spot. Keep away from there. She doesn't share it.'

'But sharing is caring,' Kenny points out.

'That is true. That's what I teach you, my baby crab, to do. But as you can see, Bertha is not a crab, and she does NOT share her spot. That's just the way crocodiles are. Now go play on the other side and don't bother big Bertha. There's plenty of room for everyone on this river,' Mummy says, firmly.

Kenny crawls over to the other side, and starts going up and down some rocks. But his eyes keep going back to Bertha.

When Mummy isn't looking, Kenny pretends to follow a leaf and moves a little closer to Bertha.

… And a little closer.

… And a little closer.

Suddenly, Bertha opens one eye. Kenny squeals and scurries back as fast as he can.

Bertha watches him run all the way to the other side. And then she smiles quietly to herself and shuts her eye.

A few days later, Kenny is back. But this time he has a plan.

He cautiously walks closer to Bertha.

… And a little closer.

… And a little closer.

Suddenly, Bertha opens one eye. Heart pounding, Kenny throws what's in his pincers on the ground and runs back as fast as he can.

Bertha watches him run back all the way to the other side. And then she smiles quietly to herself and shuts her eye.

But curiosity gets the better of Bertha. When night falls, she walks over to see what it is. 'A beaded bracelet!' Bertha exclaims. 'Such utter nonsense. Do crabs know nothing about crocodiles? What are they teaching them in school these days?' She swings her tail in anger, picks up the bracelet and throws it into the river. It makes a little splash.

The next morning, Kenny is back.

He cautiously walks closer to Bertha.

… And a little closer.

… And a little closer.

Suddenly, Bertha opens one eye. Heart pounding, Kenny throws what's in his pincers on the ground and runs back as fast as he can.

Bertha watches him run back all the way to the other side. And then she shuts her eye.

But curiosity gets the better of Bertha. When night falls, she walks over to see what it is. 'Chocolate!' Bertha exclaims. 'Seriously? Crabs know absolutely nothing about crocodiles. This is getting offensive.'

She swings her tail in disgust, picks up the chocolate and throws it into the river. It makes a little splash.

The next day, Kenny peeks at Bertha from behind the rock. Bertha opens both eyes and glares at him.

He smiles.

She glares.

He doesn't dare go closer.

A few days go by, before Kenny is back.

He cautiously walks closer to Bertha.

... And a little closer.

... And a little closer.

Suddenly, Bertha opens one eye. Heart pounding, Kenny throws what's in his pincers on the ground and runs back as fast as he can.

Bertha watches him run back all the way to the other side. Then she sees Kenny's mummy watching him from the other side. She hears her say, 'KENNY! How many times have I told you? THAT is Bertha's spot! Leave her alone. No one on the river wants an angry croc!'

Bertha shuts her eye with a little smile to herself, and a satisfied sigh. 'Moms are just the best. That should take care of that,' she whispers to herself.

But curiosity gets the better of Bertha. When night falls, she walks over to see what Kenny threw. 'A letter!' Bertha exclaims.

She reads ...

Dear Bertha,

Sharing is caring. Won't you share your spot with me? It's sunnier than any other spot by the river. And I will be quiet.

Your friend,

Kenny

Bertha is about to swing her tail in anger, but instead finds herself laughing. Her teeth sparkle in the moonlight. 'That pesky little crab,' she says to herself, as she slowly crawls back to her spot.

The next day, Kenny peeks at Bertha from behind the rock. Bertha opens both eyes and glares at him.

He smiles.

She glares.

He doesn't dare go closer.

A few days go by before Kenny is back.

He cautiously walks closer to Bertha.

... And a little closer.

... And a little closer.

Suddenly, Bertha opens one eye. Heart pounding, Kenny throws what's in his pincers on the ground and runs back as fast as he can.

Bertha watches him run back all the way to the other side. Then she hears Kenny's mummy say, 'That does it. How many times have I told you, Kenny? No more chances. You are banned from coming to this side of the river for three months. Three full months. Do you hear me?'

Bertha shuts her eye, with a little smile to herself.

But curiosity gets the better of Bertha. When night falls, Bertha walks over to see what it is. 'That's strange. I could have sworn he threw something,' says Bertha. She looks closely but still can't find anything.

The days turn into weeks, and then into months. As time passes, Bertha realizes what Kenny threw. She can see small, green leaves starting to poke out. The stems grow longer and longer, and then flowers appear!

'Seeds! That little imp threw sunflower seeds on my sunny spot by the river! Kenny grew me sunflowers. Crabs may not know anything about crocs but they do know that everyone loves sunflowers.'

Good Night, Sleep Tight!

About the Author

Nalini Sorensen is an award-winning children's author, who loves spending time with children and looking at the world through the wonder of their eyes. She believes that life is too short to not laugh, and seems to always attract highly humorous situations in her real life. She lives in Mumbai, with her husband, two sons, and dog. There is a lot of love, a lot of laughter, and *a lot* always going on in their home.

Nalini has written books across various age groups for children, and has been published by numerous publishers in India. Her book titles include, *Spellbound!*, *Lucky, It's Summer!*, *Lucky, It's Not Just a Christmas Story!*, *Lucky, It's Diwali!*, *While You Are Sleeping*, *Papa's Marathon*, *Dada's Useless Present*, *The Star That Saved the Day*, *Number March*, and *Alphabet Dress-up*. Visit **@NaliniSorensenAuthor** on Facebook or **@nalinisorensen** on Instagram to know more about her. Details of her books can be found here: **https://linktr.ee/nalinisorensen**

Other Books by Nalini Sorensen

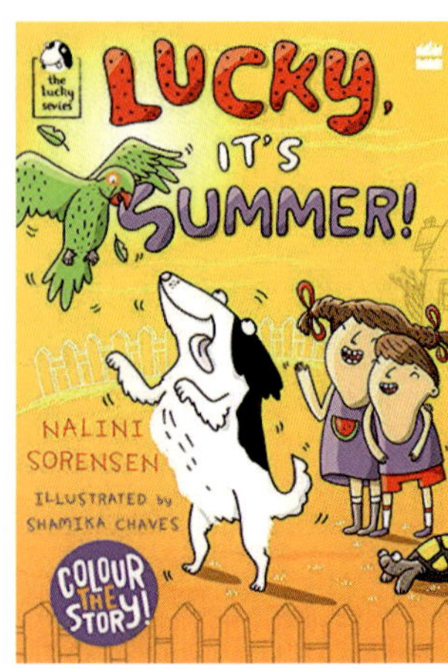

About the Illustrators

Doodlenerve is the creative duo of **Subhadeep Roy** and **Shiladitya Bose**, who have been crafting art and animation independently over the past few years. Their books include *The Tale of the Naughty Flying Mountains*, *Stories and Sutras*, *Akbar Birbal and the Haunted Gurukul*, *The Secret of Fire and Other Folktales*, *The Very, Extremely, Most Naughty Asura Tales*, *Spellbound!* and *Mythonama*. Illustrating for book publications has always been one of Doodlenerve's most favourite avenues of creativity. The duo aim to one day have a mini-library of their illustrated books! Visit **@doodlenerve** on Instagram, or **https://www.behance.net/doodlenerve**, to know more about their work.

About the Designer

Shamika Chaves is a children's book illustrator, author and graphic designer who's based in Mumbai, India. She has illustrated around twenty children's books, including those of authors like Ruskin Bond. She was nominated for Publishing Next's coveted 'Illustrator of the Year 2021' award. She lives and works in a cosy little home with her husband, Christopher, and their nine-year-old tortoise, Sebastian. Visit **@shamikasdoodles** on Instagram or **www.shamikasdoodles.com** to learn more about her work.

'*Good Night, Sleep Tight!* makes me wish I were five years old again! This collection of 21 contemporary stories and poems is packed with wisdom, humour and what-ifs. Imagine the difference we can make to our children's lives when we read them something thought-provoking right before they drift off to Dreamland!'

- Ravi Subramanian, bestselling author